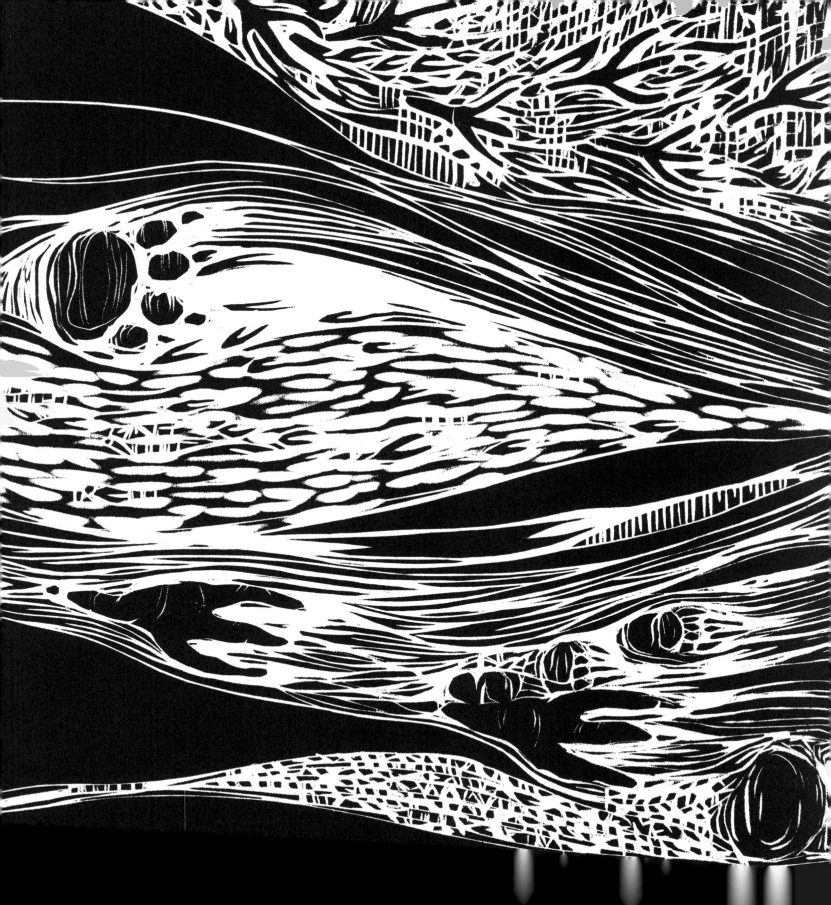

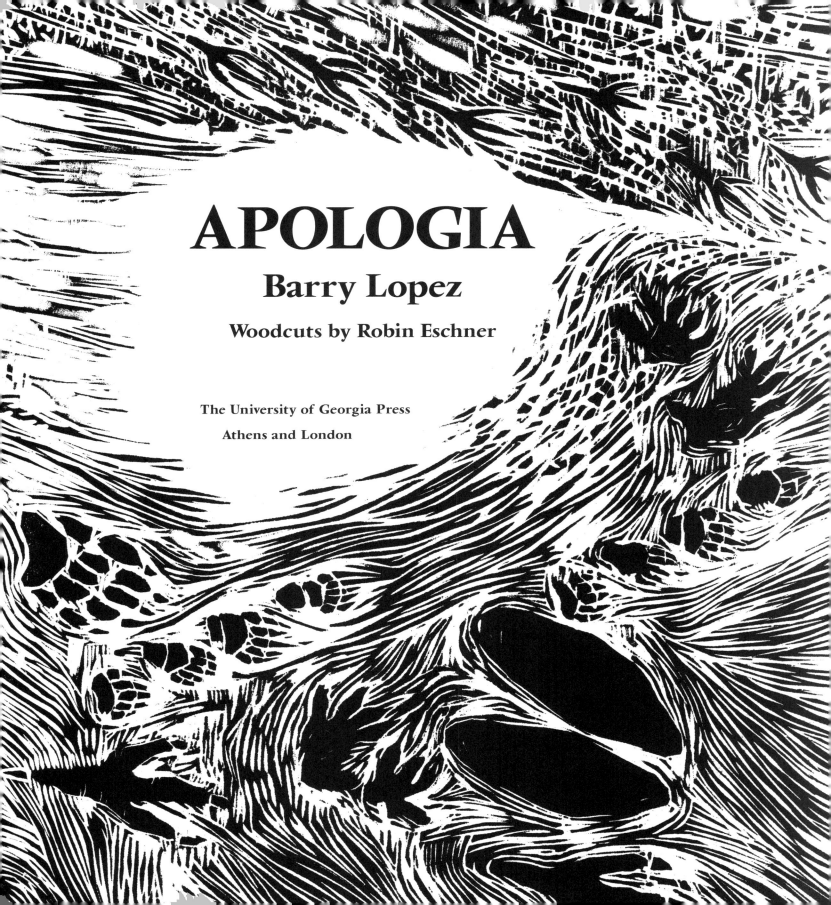

APOLOGIA

Barry Lopez

Woodcuts by Robin Eschner

The University of Georgia Press

Athens and London

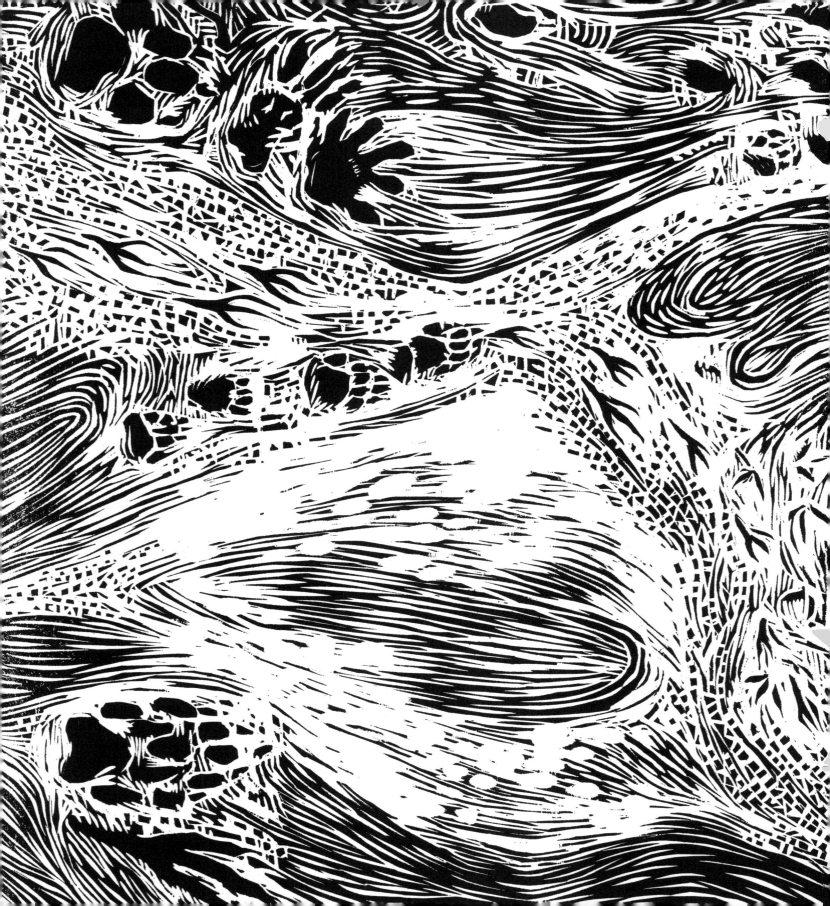

A few miles east of home

in the Cascades I slow down and pull over for
two raccoons, sprawled still as stones in the road.
I carry them to the side and lay them in sun-shot, windblown
grass in the barrow pit. In eastern Oregon, along U.S. 20,
black-tailed jackrabbits lie like welts of sod—
three, four, then a fifth. By the bridge over
Jordan Creek, just shy of the Idaho border
in the drainage of the Owyhee River, a crumpled
adolescent porcupine leers up almost maniacally
over its blood-flecked teeth. I carry each one away
from the tarmac into a cover of grass or brush
out of decency, I think. And worry.
Who are these animals, their lights gone out?
What journeys have fallen apart here?

I do not stop to remove
each dark blister from the road.
I wince before the recently
dead, feel my lips tighten,
see something else, a fence post,
in the spontaneous aversion of
my eyes, and pull over. I imagine white
silk threads of life still vibrating inside them,
even if the body's husk is stretched out for yards,
stuck like oiled muslin to the road. The energy
that once held them erect leaves like a bullet,
but the memory of that energy fades slowly from
the wrinkled cornea, the bloodless fur.

The raccoons and, later, a red fox
carry like sacks of wet gravel and sand.
Each animal is like a solitary child's shoe in the road.

Once a man asked, Why do you bother?
You never know, I said. The ones you give some
semblance of burial, to whom you offer an apology,
may have been like seers in a parallel culture.
It is an act of respect, a technique
of awareness.

In Idaho I hit a young sage sparrow—*thwack* against
the right fender in the very split second I see it. Its companion
rises from the same spot but a foot higher, slow as smoke,
and sails off clean into the desert. I rest the walloped bird in my
left hand, my right thumb pressed to its chest. I feel for the
wail of the heart. Its eyes glisten like rain on crystal.
Nothing but warmth. I shut the tiny eyelids and lay it
beside a clump of bunch grass. Beyond a barbed-wire
fence the overgrazed range is littered with cow flops.
The road curves away to the south. I nod before I go,
a disconcerted gesture, out of simple grief.

I pass four spotted skunks. The swirling air is acrid
with the rupture of each life.

Darkness rises in the valleys of Idaho. East of
Grand View, south of the Snake River, nighthawks swoop
the roads for gnats, silent on the wing as owls. On a descending
curve I see two of them lying soft as clouds in the road. I turn
around and come back. The sudden slowing down and my
K-turn at the bottom of the hill draw the attention of a
man who steps away from a tractor, a dozen yards from
where the birds lie. I can tell by his step, the suspicious
tilt of his head, that he is wary, vaguely proprietary.
Offended, or irritated, he may throw the birds back
into the road when I leave. So I wait, subdued
like a penitent, a body in each hand.

He speaks first, a low voice, a deep murmur
weighted with awe. He has been watching these flocks
feeding just above the road for several evenings. He calls them
whippoorwills. He gestures for a carcass. How odd, yes, the way
they concentrate their hunting right on the road, I say. He runs
a finger down the smooth arc of the belly and remarks on
the small whiskered bill. He pulls one long wing out straight,
but not roughly. He marvels. He glances at my car, baffled by
this out-of-state courtesy. Two dozen nighthawks careen past,
back and forth at arm's length, feeding at our height and lower.
He asks if I would mind—as though I owned it—if he took
the bird up to the house to show his wife. "She's never seen
anything like this." He's fascinated. "Not close."

I trust, later, he will put it in the fields, not throw the body
in the trash, a whirligig.

North of Pinedale

in western Wyoming on U.S. 189, below the Gros Ventre Range,
I see a big doe from a great distance, the low rays of first light gleaming
in her tawny reddish hair. She rests askew, like a crushed tree.
I drag her to the shoulder, then down a long slope by the petals of
her ears. A gunny sack of plaster mud, ears cold as rain gutters.
All of her doesn't come. I climb back up for the missing leg.
The stain of her is darker than the black asphalt. The stains
go north and off to the south as far as I can see.

On an afternoon trafficless, quiet as a cloister, headed across
South Pass in the Wind River Range, I swerve violently but hit a bird
and then try to wrestle the gravel-spewing skid in a straight line
along the lip of an embankment. I know even as I struggle for
control the irony of this: I could pitch off here to my own
death, easily. The bird is dead somewhere in the road behind me.
Only a few seconds and I am safely back on the road,
nauseated, lightheaded.

It is hard to distinguish among
younger gulls. I turn this one around slowly
in my hands. It could be a western gull,
a mew gull, a California gull. I do not
remember well enough the bill markings,
the color of the legs. I have no doubt about
the vertebrae shattered beneath the
seamless white of its ropy neck.

East of Lusk, Wyoming,
in Nebraska, I stop for a badger.
I squat on the macadam to admire
the long claws, the perfect set of its
teeth in the broken jaw, the ramulose
shading of its fur—how it differs
slightly, as does every badger's,
from the drawings and pictures
in the field guides. A car drifts
toward us over the prairie,
coming on in the other lane,
a white 1962 Chevrolet station wagon.
The driver slows to pass.
In the bright sunlight I can't see
his face, only an arm and the gesture
of his thick left hand. It opens in a
kind of shrug, hangs briefly in
limp sadness, then extends itself
in supplication. Gone past,
it curls into itself against
the car door and is still.

Farther on in western Nebraska
I pick up the small bodies of mice and birds.
While I wait to retrieve these creatures I do not meet
the eyes of passing drivers. Whoever they are, I feel anger
toward them, in spite of the sparrow and the gull I myself
have killed. We treat the attrition of lives on the road like
the attrition of lives in war: horrifying, unavoidable, justified.
Accepting the slaughter leaves people momentarily
fractious, embarrassed. South of Broken Bow, at dawn,
I cannot avoid an immature barn swallow.
It hangs by its head, motionless
in the slats of the grille.

I stop for a rabbit on Nebraska 806 and find,
only a few feet away, a garter snake. What else have I missed,
too small, too narrow? What has gone under or past me
while I stared at mountains, hay meadows, fencerows,
the beryl surface of rivers? In Wyoming I could not help
but see pronghorn antelope swollen big as barrels by the side
of the road, their legs splayed rigidly aloft. For animals
so large people will stop. But how many have this habit of
clearing the road of smaller creatures, people who
would remove the ones I miss? I do not imagine
I am alone. As much sorrow as the man's
hand conveyed in Nebraska, it meant
gratitude too for burying the dead.

Still, I do not wish to meet anyone's eyes.

In southwestern Iowa, outside Clarinda,
I haul a deer into high grass out of sight of the road
and begin to examine it. It is still whole, but the
destruction is breathtaking. The skull, I soon discover,
is fractured in four places; the jaw, hanging by shreds
of mandibular muscle, is broken at the symphysis,
beneath the incisors. The pelvis is crushed,
the left hind leg unsocketed. All but two ribs are
dislocated along the vertebral column, which is complexly
fractured. The intestines have been driven forward
into the chest. The heart and lungs have ruptured
the chest wall at the base of the neck.
The signature of a tractor-trailer truck:
80,000 pounds at 65 mph.

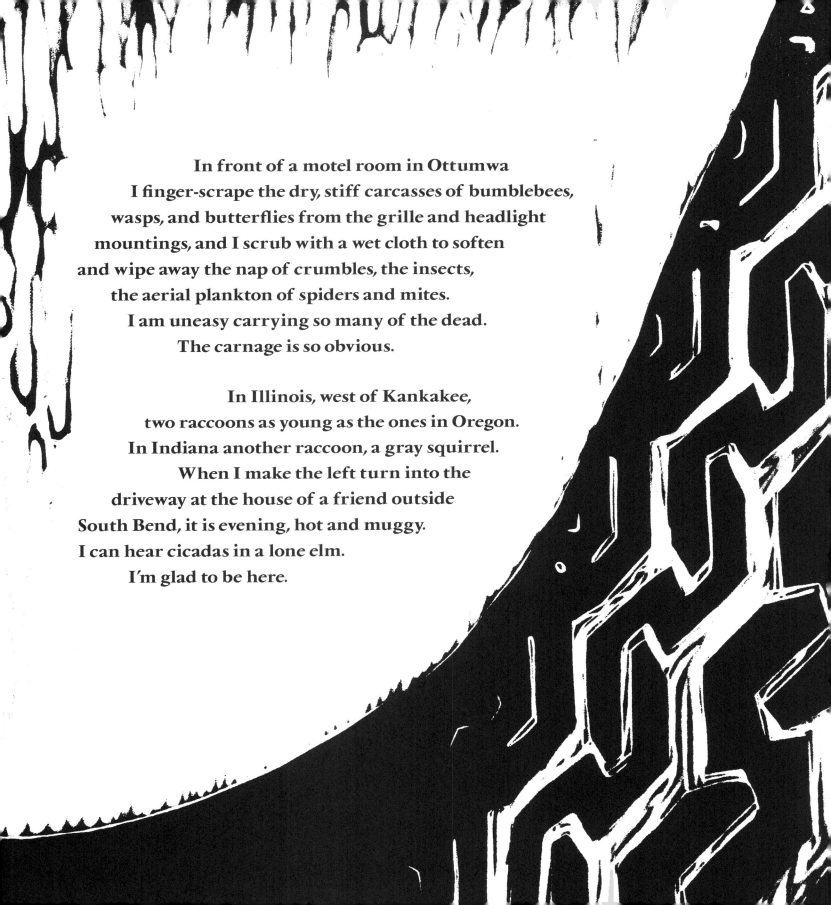

In front of a motel room in Ottumwa
I finger-scrape the dry, stiff carcasses of bumblebees,
wasps, and butterflies from the grille and headlight
mountings, and I scrub with a wet cloth to soften
and wipe away the nap of crumbles, the insects,
the aerial plankton of spiders and mites.
I am uneasy carrying so many of the dead.
The carnage is so obvious.

In Illinois, west of Kankakee,
two raccoons as young as the ones in Oregon.
In Indiana another raccoon, a gray squirrel.
When I make the left turn into the
driveway at the house of a friend outside
South Bend, it is evening, hot and muggy.
I can hear cicadas in a lone elm.
I'm glad to be here.

From the driveway entrance I look
back down Indiana 23, toward Indiana 8,
remembering the farm roads of Illinois
and Iowa. I remember how beautiful it was
in the limpid air to drive Nebraska 2
through the Sand Hills, to see how far at dusk
the land was etched east and west of
Wyoming 28. I remember the imposition
of the Wind River Range in a hard, blue sky
beneath white ranks of buttonhook clouds,
windy hay fields on the Snake River Plain,
the welcome of Russian olive trees and willows
in western creek bottoms. The transformation
of the heart such beauty engenders is not
enough tonight to let me shed the heavier
memory, a catalog too morbid to write out,
too vivid to ignore.

I stand in the driveway now,
   listening to the cicadas whirring in the dark tree.
    My hands grip the sill of the open window at the driver's side,
and I lean down as if to speak to someone still sitting there.
    The weight I wish to fall I cannot fathom, a sorrow over the
      world's dark hunger.

    A light comes on over the porch. I hear a deadbolt thrown,
the shiver of a door pulled free. The words of atonement
I pronounce are too inept to offer me release. Or forgiveness.
    My friend is floating across the tree-shadowed lawn.
      What is to be done with the desire for exculpation?

    "Later than we thought you'd be," he says.
I do not want the lavabo. I wish to make amends.
    "I made more stops than I thought I would," I answer.
      "Well, bring in your things. And whatever
        I can take," he offers.

I anticipate, in the powerful antidote
of our conversation, the reassurance of a human enterprise,
the forgiving embrace of the rational. It waits within,
beyond the slow tail-wagging of two dogs
standing at the screen door.

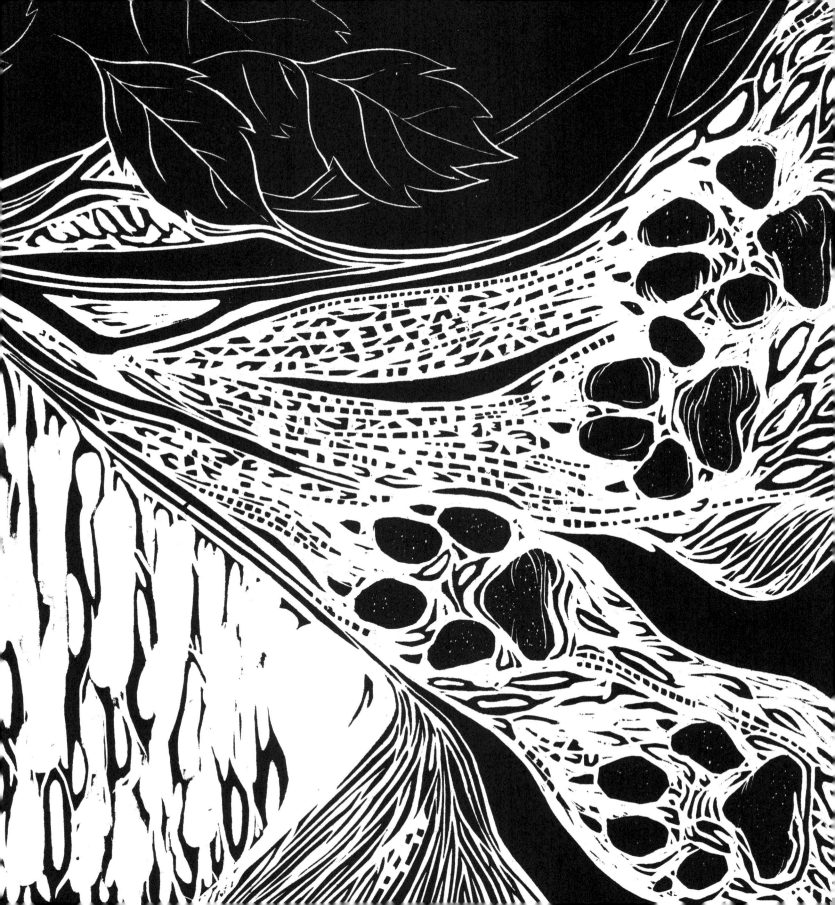

Published by the University of Georgia Press
Athens, Georgia 30602
Copyright © 1998 by Barry Holstun Lopez and Robin Eschner
"Apologia" copyright © 1989, 1997 by Barry Holstun Lopez
Illustrations copyright © 1997 by Robin Eschner
All rights reserved
Designed by Erin Kirk New
Set in 12.5 on 20 Vendôme
Printed and bound in Canada by Friesens
The paper in this book meets the guidelines for permanence and durability
of the Committee on Production Guidelines for Book Longevity
of the Council on Library Resources.

02 01 00 99 98 C 5 4 3 2 1

Library of Congress Cataloging in Publication Data

Lopez, Barry Holstun, 1945–
Apologia / Barry Lopez ; woodcuts by Robin Eschner.
p. cm.
Originally published: Eugene Or. : Lone Goose Press, 1997.
ISBN 0-8203-2004-8 (alk. paper)
1. Roadkills—United States—Anecdotes. 2. Lopez, Barry Holstun, 1945–
—Journeys—United States. I. Eschner, Robin. II. Title.
QL155.L66 1998
818'.5403—dc21
[B]
97-43117

Previously published by lone goose press, Eugene, Oregon,
in April 1997 in a limited edition of fifty signed and
numbered books. Designed by Charles Hobson.
Production coordinated by Charles Hobson,
in collaboration with Barry Lopez, Robin Eschner,
publisher and box maker Sandy Tilcock,
letterpress printer Susan Acker,
edition printer Nora Pauwels,
and binder John DeMerritt.